INSPIRED

BOOK 1

NANCY EHRENFELD

ISBN 979-8-88616-647-7 (paperback)
ISBN 979-8-88616-648-4 (digital)

Christian Faith Publishing
832 Park Avenue
Meadville, PA 16335
www.christianfaithpublishing.com

Printed in the United States of America

Contents

These THOUGHTS are of a sixteen-year-old teen. Growing, wishing, and hoping for the future. A junior in high school; her whole life ahead of her. The beginning of her writings. Written between January 1965 and June 1965.

The Little Things

January 11, 1965

At this hour of the night
When there is but little light;
I look up at the stars and see
The little things that are to me
Most valuable, for they appear
At lonely times when no one's near.

These little things that make me think
Of wondrous thoughts and countless dreams
Are oh-so very comforting
Because they bring me everything.

A Friend

January 11, 1965

I'll treasure his friendship,
I'll remember his words;
And still, we'll have fun
Just like little birds
At play on a branch
Of a mighty tree.
And also like all the fishes in the sea.

Our friendship will grow
Until one day we'll part.
But always he'll be
Somewhere in my heart.
For his kindness and pureness sing out like a lark.
And always he'll be somewhere in my heart.

A Bulging Stomach

I had too much to eat today!
That's why I feel this way.

And so it's nice to lie in bed
And sleep the day away.

While all the while the angels say,
"You had too much to eat today,

So lay in bed and sleep, sleep, sleep;
Sleep the day away!

And in the morning when you wake,
Finally rid of this dread fate,

You'll eat again and feel the same.
So what's the use in playing a game?

Do as you please and you will see
That playing games is not for thee."

The Friend—II

March 10, 1965

That friend who used to be only a mere acquaintance,
Is now the one with whom I make my appointments.

We have more fun than in the past
Because we realize at last

That we two need each other's arm
To keep us from all evil harm.

We need to grow in mind AND soul,
Until we finally reach our goal;

Whatever it may be.

My Love

April 30, 1965

I have a love that none can know.

My love is always white as snow.

When he is with me, we are as one.

When we are apart, we are as none.

He's been away, but when he comes.

I'll show him love as bright as the sun.

I'll show him that I really care.

And all my love with him I'll share.

When My Guy Returns

April 30, 1965

On the road to somewhere
There is a touch so kind.

It makes one feel so cherished
I'm oh-so glad it's mine.

And when this one of whom I speak
Is finally at my door.

I'll run to him with open arms
And leave him nevermore.

But if this love of mine should stop,
And never reach my door.

I'd never love another soul.
For I would BE no more!

The End of a Story

May 3, 1965

The flower bloomed

And showed all its glory.

Now the flower is dead,

And the end of a story.

June 7, 1965

The new bend in the road—

Is ONE nice turn.

I've only traveled it a short time.

But from what I've seen,

The asphalt really shines!

June 7, 1965

The dead flower bloomed.

But, seeing no other flower,

It wilted away.

For you see, the other flower

Was behind a stone—

And there it would stay.

June 11, 1965

I had a dream long, long ago.

This dream was so real that no one knows.

How bad it hurts to realize

That all it was, was childish lies.

Not lies of meanness or lies of scorn.

But all these lies weren't meant to harm

As they did.

June 11, 1965

The cave of bats; one was blind, the other scared as a rat.

Blind bats can't see; they need a key for every door.

Scared bats are blind too; but these creatures

Dream dreams galore.

Scared bats worry about these impossible dreams.

Dreams of one day flying out of the Nigger cave.

Looking at the blind bat and laughing;

Not worrying anymore.

But this, it seems, will never happen.

For this one scared bat needs a key for all doors.

Sometime after 1971 but before 1980

To My Mother-in-Law

Nobody has an in-law like you.
A mother, grandma, and mother-in-law, too!

A genuine person who forgives and forgets.
A person who catches each day in a net.

And lets it all out as you need to do.
For you never really are finally through

With all that is asked and taken away
From you who are strong, and here to stay.

I cannot find nary a flaw
Thanks for being my Mother-in-law

      Love, Nancy

May 26, 1980

Another year has passed again
Do you believe that's true?
And still, I say I'm glad to have
A mother-in-law like you!

You wash my clothes, you clean my house;
You watch the kids all day.
I thank you for the love you give
And hope, along the way

That someday I can do the things
That come naturally to you.
For maybe someday, I myself
Will be a mother-in-law, too!

Love,
Nancy

Happy Birthday

September 21, 1980

God bless you on your special day.
He's helped you come this long, long way.
Through thick and thin, and ups and downs.
And recently even twenty pounds!

Thirty-four summers you've seen go by.
Thirty-four winters have covered the sky.
And all of the things that have passed your way
Have made you what you are today;

A father, a lover, a friend, don't you see?
So have a good day,

Rikki, Joey, and Me
"We love you!"

God Grabbing Me—
Pulling Me to Him

I had a humbling experience in 1980–1981, December to January. It started with increasing double vision followed by involuntary eye movement. The ophthalmologist said, "Too much stress in your workplace." I was a nurse in ICU. Loved it. "Take some time off," he said. That only CAUSED stress. No other symptoms. No headache. No dizziness. I just saw two of everything and everyone and had to continually refocus because of involuntary eye movement. The neurologist consultation ruled out various neurological conditions. He wanted a CT scan of the cerebellum (the lower portion of the brain called the small brain). Our hospital CT only scanned the upper portion of the brain, the cerebrum.

So off to the University of Miami to Jackson Memorial Hospital I went for a neurosurgeon consultation. Conclusion: no tumor, no disease. Only Arnold-Chiari malformation. The "tonsils" of my cerebellum had "dropped" into the foramen magnum. That's the hole in the floor of the skull that allows the spinal cord and cranial nerves to leave the brain, thus compressing some of the cranial nerves.

As the poems indicate, even before we knew the outcome, everything turned out just fine. The surgeon removed my occipital skull bone, thus widening the space for the tonsils, nerves, and the like. He also performed a laminectomy of cervical one and two of the spine bones where they connect to the skull.

God planned each step of the above chapter of my life. And He walked right through it with me. He also pulled my husband in to show him His power and awesomeness! Oh, by the way, the double vision and involuntary eye movement? GONE.

December 14, 1980—written from my hospital bed in Jackson
Memorial Hospital, Miami, Florida

—Nancy Ehrenfeld

Tonight, I'm sort of anxious
And my mind is going fast.

I've got to make myself remember
To let this be God's task.

If I put myself in His loving arms
I know He'll hold me gently.

Then I can thank Him afterward
That I'm awfully glad He sent me—

On the road to recovery
Where I will forget Him never!

And home to friends and family
Where He will reign forever!

Written the morning of December 15, 1980, from the eighth-
floor surgical waiting room in Jackson Memorial Hospital, Miami,
Florida.

—Laura Hooker

God and we are waiting,
Here in this little room.

Bob, Dad, and I are hoping,
We'll hear about you soon.

We've silently said our special prayers,
And felt His calming hand.

We know you will recover,
And things will be just grand.

God is ever with you.
You have a lot of faith.

By Christmas, you'll be well again.
Back at home and safe.

—Love, Mother

December 15, 1980, 1:30 p.m.
In the hall, eighth floor

Now we've heard the good news
And we're rid of all our "blues."

We can soon get off our seats
AND finally go and eat.

We can tell them all at home
That you won't ever be alone.

God will be there, your room to share
In the intensive care.

But not for long,
Let's sing a song!

—Daddy and Mother

An Empty ICU—May 28, 1983

Here I sit with beds around me.
Not a human being to find.
All twelve bedspreads smooth and neat.
Not a symptom nor a sign.

Memories fill my whirling head.
Faces, figures all combined.
Pain and suffering, joy and gladness.
Many names and thoughts I find.

Just the hum of air-conditioning.
The motor of the ice machine.
Once in a while, the pipes go *clank*.
And heat cracks walls but goes unseen.

I feel a closeness to this unit.
We've been through some pretty trying times.
At last, it has a chance to tell me
Exactly what's on its mind.

This unit has heard every word.
Twenty-four hours a day.
This unit has seen every face.
From 1965 until today.

It really is awesome to think about.
The many stories it holds.
And pretty soon, another will come
But the stories still go untold.

And thirty-eight years later as I work in Same-Day Surgery, just outside the ICU, the stories still go "UNTOLD."

Mother's Day

To both my moms this Mother's Day
Of nineteen eighty-four.
You're both the best in every way.
You've got the highest score.

Mother H. so small and slight;
How well you cared for me.
You taught me all the right from wrong.
How I ought to be.

You raised me from a little girl
To what I am today.
You showed me that you love me
With very little to say.

I was last in line with your babies.
Your attention was already spent.
But we got our time together
When the other two babies went.

And now, today, I owe you more
Than I can ever repay.
I just want you to know that I love you
In a very special way!

And now for Mother E.
That other girl in my life.
I thank you for all the patience you show
During quite a lot of my strife.

We've known each other for nineteen years,
And I think I've told you just once.
But let me tell you again and again,
"I love you a whole, whole bunch"

You put up with a lot.
I'll never know how you do it.
And it always seems what'er the result;
That somehow you already knew it.

They call it "woman's intuition."
But I think it's special to you.
That quiet, calm, cool knowledge
That always sees you through!

And now dear mothers, I want to add
Just one more closing line.
If I can be just a little of both,
As a mother, I'll do fine.

—Love, Nancy

Father's Day

Year—possibly the 1990s?

You are my father, yes, indeed.
I've loved you from the start.
You've worked and slaved and toiled to succeed.
You'll always be in my heart.

I remember happy times.
I remember sad times too.
When you would get the plastic belt
To teach us a thing or two.

One time I set out selling Christmas cards,
I hated every minute.
When I came home without a dime.
You said, "The police will decide your limit!"

When I burst out crying, you hugged me tight.
And said you were only kidding.
You didn't care about any cards.
That you didn't mind me quitting.

Remember when you got that mask;
And snuck outside at night?
We'd be taking a bath and playing around,
Then we'd be scared to death with fright! Ha!

I'll never forget while riding along,
With everyone in the car.
My sourball got stuck in my throat.
So you flipped me and it flew out—far!

Being the youngest one of three,
I had to share your love.
Oh, jealous I'd get, that's normal you see.
But I knew you would have enough.

Remember the fishing sinkers you made?
Where did you get all that silver?
On the back porch of Glenwood, it was.
I was always amazed and bewildered!

And then you invented the tackle box.
The one that was really a chair.
You worked really hard; hours passed on the clock.
There was nothing else that could compare.

You and Mother were always there
To cheer me on as I danced.
To believe in me too; and in all I could do.
You continually gave me that chance.

Thank you for walking me down the aisle.
That meant so much to me.
You gave me away after nineteen years,
To let me get down from your knee.

Well, now I would like to thank you again.
And dance a little twirl.
I love you a lot;
And you're never "forgot."

Happy Father's Day
—Your little girl!

Death of a Father-in-Law

God influences my writings more and more.

May 1999
Read at Ray Ehrenfeld's
Funeral Service

He may have yelled; he may have fought.
And he never ever gave it a thought.

He loved his mom, he loved his dad;
Even though sometimes things got bad.

Brother Bill, Brother Clyde
One was shrewd, the other sly.

Married he got when he was young.
That didn't last, but he had one son.

Raised him he did 'til he was ten;
Then he fell in love and married again.

This time Juanita was the love of his life.
Mother of their six and a beautiful wife.

Ray worked hard all of his days.
But that old devil alcohol guided his ways.

Carousing and fighting and acting insane,
Don't mix with a family that's hungry and tame.

Don't get me wrong, there were good times, too.
Like fishing and hunting and picnicking; it's true!

But kids getting older, marrying now;
After twenty-nine years, Pop just left—somehow.

It was hard for the "kids" and Mom, of course, too.
We don't understand all we have to go through.

Ray carried on, still bowling a lot.
He was with Dottie now; and three other tots.

Working hard building; constructing many additions,
He taught Robert exactly to nail to perfection.

He was strong and hard as a rock.
He'd fall off a roof and go get the next block.

But years took their toll, they sneaked up so fast.
Ray had to slow down to glance at the past.

In a wheelchair with oxygen for some months now.
We'd go out to dinner, and he'd just keep getting thinner.

Three weeks ago, he requested a place
Where he ate his whole meal and enjoyed the sun race.

It raced to the edge of the water so blue.
Then it winked at him and said, "I'll see you real soon."

He told us that he had kneeled down by his bed
To ask God's forgiveness; then bowed his head.

You know how hard of hearing he was; yet near to the end,
Thursday night, I swear, he heard every word of Larry's prayer.

Larry prayed to the Father of all of us here
To take Ray with ease and without any fear.

Then he told Pop to go, it was "OK" now.
Your family says so and God will allow.

So he closed his eyes and took a breath.
Calmly and quietly, Ray Ehrenfeld left.

So I really believe that my father-in-law, Ray
Received Christ in his heart before going away.

And he'll be in heaven when we get there
Because Jesus died on that cross for our sins to bear.

Christmas—1999

In a house on Harbor in '68;
That's where this story begins.
It was Christmas time, the tree was aglow.
There were lots of family and friends.

A few years later, it was Sunninglow.
Ithica, Deedra, and Albury, too.
Six little kids had grown up, you know;
And life was starting anew!

Every year, there seemed to be more.
Always a baby around.
We opened presents and ate 'till we burst.
Planning next year's round. (Whose house?)

And now we're here at Fullerton.
No more grandpa's on Christmas Eve.
The decorations all over the place.
I wonder if he can see?

The manger scenes are my favorite ones,
Joseph, Mary, and Babe.
The shepherds, wise men, camels, and sheep
Around the stable, they gaze.

And don't forget the Christmas tree;
For what it represents.
It's not just for the ornaments
And the gifts that everyone sent.

Think of the tree used long ago
With branches straight and strong.
That held that precious baby boy,
But not for very long.

Now "look" at the tree without the nail.
Not even a sign of a hole.
And you've just imagined in your mind
The cross; without the toll!

The price was paid that day on the hill
So we can celebrate—
His birth, His life, His death, His rise
To His Father's Golden Gate.

And here we go again today,
Thinking of next year's climb.
Another place, another stop
In this family's journey in time.
(See you at Tom and Jen's)

Tara, our future daughter-in-law, married our youngest son, Joe, on November 2, 2002. A future mother-in-law's prayer.

August 31, 2002, to Tara

When you wake up in the morning
Greet him with a smile,
No matter how you feel.
You'll really be in style.

Then open up your Bible
And read God's word of affection.
He'll get you going on your way
And in the right direction.

Now you're ready for a run;
At least a country mile.
You'll feel so good about yourself,
You might even "blade" awhile.

Now you're ready to get to work
After some breakfast, of course!
So off you go in your neat little car.
The Father, your reliable source.

Throughout your day, you'll think of Joe
And talk to him, I'm sure!
You'll do your work and do it well.
The day will go by like a BLUR!

Marriage will have its ups and its downs.
And all kinds of crazy things.
But always remember to look at your hand
And concentrate on that little ring.

It's a circle that doesn't stop.
A never-ending line.
It's called LOVE; and LOVE never fails.
It's always, always KIND!

The day is done
And so are the dishes.
You're tired and sleepy
But you both have wishes. (Go for it!)

Then get on your knees and thank the Lord
That HE brought you two together.
And thank Him for today.
And tell Him, "It couldn't get any BETTER!"

Love,
Your mother-in-law Nancy

Our oldest son, single, dating, and searching for his future, blessed us with a beautiful baby granddaughter on February 25, 1994. Her mother asked Robert and me if we wanted to be a part of her life. Beyond that, she asked if we would give her her middle name. Their family tradition is to be called by their middle name. She informed us that her first name was going to be Deborah.

Robert named our first boy. He didn't want teachers calling out "Richard," so he spelled it Rikki. No confusion or guessing. So years earlier, we had planned for our second child, right? A cute little girl named Nikki. Well, God had HIS plan all along, and out popped little "Joey." So the story ended. OR DID IT?

Since we didn't get OUR girl, we chose to name our granddaughter Nicole—to be called "Nikki." And ten very fast years later, this tribute was written for her.

Terrific 10

February 28, 2004

Nikki's tenth
Birthday
Feb 25, 2004

She's ten years old now
I can't believe it!
She's grown and grown
I can't perceive it!

That tiny chunky baby girl
Has beautiful hair now,
But not one curl.

She's got the eyebrows
Of a model-to-be.
And lashes so long
She can hardly see!

Her blue eyes will melt you
As they gaze into yours.
And her nose. What a nose!
It has just the right curves.

And then there are her lips.
So full and so pink.
She doesn't need lipstick
To make your heart sink!

Her ears they're just great.
They hear every word.
They've been pierced three times
Someday a fourth time, I'm sure!

A tiny dot you can see by her eye.
A beauty mark maybe?
No, a pencil lead too nigh!

Her teeth, well, here's a story about them.
They were perfect and white and straight as a pin
Until the "seesaw" got her one day at school.
But fret not, the orthodontist she has is so cool
He'll fix up her "bite"
So she can smile just right!

Let's get to her legs.
Now they are some "beauts"
So long slim and shapely
She'll buy extra-long suites!

The rest of her body
Is put together just right.
Arms, hands, and feet,
They all fit real tight!

And don't forget her buttocks.
It's so cute you know.
Up where her legs start
"Just watch it go!"

Next is her mind.
Always going so fast.
She'd better slow down
Or she'll miss the past!

Her brain's like a sponge
Always soaking up more.
But when she's lost interest
Oh, what a chore.

It is to stay focused
On the here and now
With everything all at once
Can't wait—don't know how!

Now for my favorite
Part of her yet.
The part that makes
All the others second best.

This part of Nikki
Will always be there.
You can't take it!
Can't hide it
But with it, you'll share.

You'll share her love.
You'll share her soul.
You'll share the heart
That makes her whole.

Love, Grandma Nancy

Written sometime in late 2003 or early 2004

There is a cool family.
Their name will come later.
They live in Plant City,
Home of the famous "Tater" (NOT)
        You know it's the strawberry!

This dad and this mom
Fell in deep, deep love.
She single and lonely,
He sent from above.

Five kids are "theirs" now.
Not his or not hers.
Some "ins" and some "outs"
And a couple of swerves.

Their house is a "home."
They've made it that way.
Scraping and painting;
Or SOMETHING all day!

He works very hard
In creating rooms.
She welcomes her patrons
And manages to the moon!

And now for their names
From bottom to top.
Carson, Devyn, Sidney, Nikki, Caitlin.
None of them swap.

Dad is Rik, and
Mom is Bobbiejo.
The Ehrenfelds are ready
To move into that home!

And most important;
What keeps their great behavior?
They ALL know Jesus,
And know He's their Savior!

Rik then married Bobbiejoe on July 10, 2004

Written on May 9, 2004, for Mother's Day

My mother is short but very tall.
She's very large, yet seems so small!

I remember looking UP at her.
She was so high, her face was a blur.

She fed me, clothed me, loved me,
Molded me into another—mother.

She showed me how to love a man.
No matter how hard or what is at hand.

By staying beside him each and every day.
Through thick and thin, showing love all the way.

She was praying for me though I didn't know it.
Until I realized her life was what showed it!

She introduced me to my Heavenly Father.
I saw in her strength, her will, and her honor—to Him.

She's really a giant in a tiny frame.
There's no one else like her.

So of course her name is—MOTHER!

THE TREE—Hurricane Charley visited us on August 13, 2004. This story relates the ravaged oaks in our yard to our Christmas Tree.

The Tree—2004

The oaks were tall and stately.
They covered our yard completely.
Planted when the house was built.
They grew and grew so sweetly.

Robert's pride and joy
Along with his two boys.
He watered and watered those beautiful trees.
They never made a noise.

Eighteen years from small to big.
Eighteen years from thin to thick.
Eighteen years he watched them grow.
Eighteen years and the branches bowed!

Now—the tree we have this Christmas
Shows God's amazing plans.
This branch still hanging by a thread.
With all this green it stands.

There was a tree long, long ago.
With broken branches, too.
It covered lots of ground also.
Until it became—just TWO.

Two boards shaped into a perfect *T*.
It might have been an oak.
It might have been just like this one.
For a cross to hang His cloak.

Our tree swayed with a hurricane.
Back and forth it went.
His tree was still and straight and tall.
To hold His body—bent.

It held His body with those nails.
Until all life was gone.
Until all sin was washed away.
And to Him, we all belong!

See the birds? The new green leaves?
Our oak is coming back.
It's standing tall, the way He did
When out of the cave of black—
        He came!

Nurse Nancy was one of the first. She started here in 1970, and she surely wasn't the worst.

Her first department was ICU; now she works in ACC and likes that too.

Bringing smiles, hugs, and kindness is always her way; she is always willing to help each and every day.

Running around the unit wearing pigtails, her hair never gets in the way when she's listening to rhonchi and rales (*lung sounds that is*).

In the afternoon, she is ready in a snap all because, on her lunch break, she took a little nap.

Fruit, fruit, that's all she eats. Oranges, apples, but *never* sweets.

Eight hours of work doesn't wear her down; you'll always see her out jogging across the other end of town.

A few years back, she won nurse of the year; we all stood up and gave a cheer.

Being a spiritual person is her way; with patients and employees, she will stand and pray.

Her seven grandkids are a big part of her life; she's a devoted grandmother and a loving wife.

Years down the road when you're retired and sitting in your cabin in North Carolina, don't worry about us; we'll be soon behind ya.

We love you and appreciate you, and that's a fact. God bless you and love you from the ACC pack.

KUDOS to Nancy for thirty-five years!

Written by Dana Bivens and Kari Stolte with help from Sue Paulson, Lindsay Cooper, JJ Juliano, Lyn Peters, Sherry Faulk, and Pat Grimmett.

2006—thirty-five-year anniversary at CRMC

Our cat, Perilandra, disappeared one day and never returned. One of her favorite spots was across the street to a wooded lot. New construction became apparent, so her special place was invaded. Robert felt so sad and sorry for me; he went to the Humane Society and surprised me on my next birthday.

Ode to a Cat

She came into my life from my husband so sweet.
It was easy to see, she liked him more than me.

Twenty-three toes stuck out from her feet.
Thus, her name "23" for a cat so complete.

Muted calico; the papers read.
Three months old and ready to be fed.

At six months old, we got her fixed.
We'd had enough of litters and kits.

Loving was strictly all on her terms.
When she made the move—here came the "purrs."

At fourteen years old, she was thin by now.
But had a good appetite—like a cow!

Snack time with Robert, she loved the most.
Front paws on his couch, her eyes on the "dose."

Of chips and Fritos and cookies and such,
"Crunch, crunch," came the sound with each little munch.

"Inside—outside" was her type.
Asleep on the couch or wandering all night.

One day at work in 2004
A hurricane hit; I could say a lot more!

But since then, I've wondered and wanted to ask,
"23," just where did you go, and how did you last?

With trees falling every which way in her sight
She probably hung on with all of her might!

We didn't see her; started feeling real sad.
Then there she was again; you could tell she was glad.

We thank God on the day you lay down on the ground.
Not a scratch or a bruise or a cut to be found.

We bid you "Goodbye," dug a grave nice and deep.
Gently carried you there to continue your sleep.

A short time later, I stepped outside
And there was your friend to bid you "goodbye."

The young Tabby; dark gray, with white on his chest
Was sitting there quietly doing his best

Not to cry. But to thank you for being his pal,
And sharing your life with him for a while.

Written 2007/2008

These *A*-to-*Z* poems were all written in conjunction with illus-trated books. They should be somewhere in close proximity to this notebook. Written probably between 2004 and 2008.

Below are two illustrated examples.

A

Is for apple—have you ever had one baked?

B

Is for bread—you can have it, and it's great!

A to Z—No "C"

There are many, many diets
In this world to review.

Here's just one more little one
That will make you feel new!

A is for Apple—have you ever had one baked?
B is for Bread—you CAN have it, and it's great!
       Remember no "C"
D is for Delicious, Delectable Dills.
E is for Eggplant growing on hills. (Also, for exercise—the kind that
    heals.)
F is for Flavor that comes from them all.
G is for Goodness that makes us grow tall.
H for the Health nut you're turning into.
I for the Ice cube that makes us so cool!
J for the Jazzy meals you will make.
K for the "Kalories" that you will shake.
L for the Lifestyle change in your future.
M for your Muscles that won't need a suture.
N for those chewy, homemade Noodles.
O for the people shouting, "Oodles."
P for the Perfect table you set.
Q for the Quickness in your step.
R for the Roast that's in the pot.
S for the String beans you'll like a lot.
T for the ripe red Tomatoes all sliced.
U for the Ukulele playing so nice.

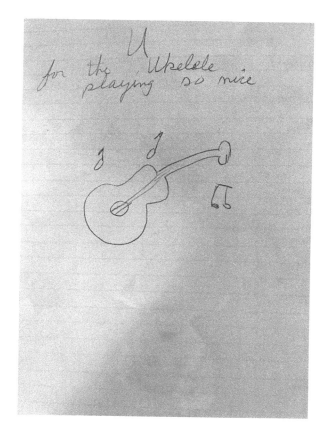

U for the Ukelele playing so nice

V for the Victory you will feel.
W for the Weight you will lose with each meal.
X for the X-tra food you will eat.
Y for the Yellow bananas so sweet.
And Z for this Zany book—so complete.

What's that you say? This book's not complete?
Oh, yeah! I forgot all those C's in a heap!

C is for Candy—should not enter your mouth.
C is for Cookies—they make your body go south.
C is for Cake—yike! We know what that does.
C is for Crackers—all kinds, that's the buzz.

53

C is for Cheese—by itself or with any.
C is for Coke—that will make you uncanny.
C is for Chips—they make your hips poke (out).

When you've got a handle
On mind over matter.

A little splurge with a "C"
Will make you feel gladder.

All this can be done
By the strength from above.

Eat daily with God
And drink in His love!

A to Z—No "D"

Sometimes we have to be on our backs to look up.

A is for Angry—that's OK to be.

B is for Breaking the fury in me.
C for the Coping I'm learning to do.
Remember no "D"
E for the Excuses I've made to you.
F for the Forgiveness that will come.
G for the Goodness that I have won.
H for the Haziness of the past.
I for the Injury that will not last.
J for the Jesus that I lean on.

K for His Kindness—like a soothing song.
L for the Life that is in me again.
M for My Many wonderful friends.

N for the Nurturing time that heals.
O for the Openness that my heart feels.
P for the many Prayers that were said.
Q for the Quiet times in my bed.
R for the Rest my body has now.
S for the Settled heart—I don't hear a sound.
T for the Tender love of my Father.
U for the Union of one heart to another.
V for the Victory over my sadness.
W for Wellness that brings about gladness.
X for the X-tra time that it takes.

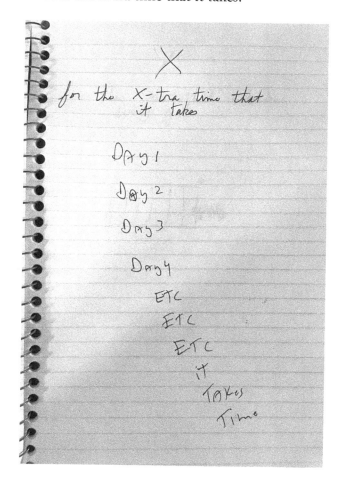

Y for the "Yes" that unlocks every gate.
And Z for the puzzled look on your face!

What about "D" you ask?
Oh, that's for "Depression."
Remember that's out;

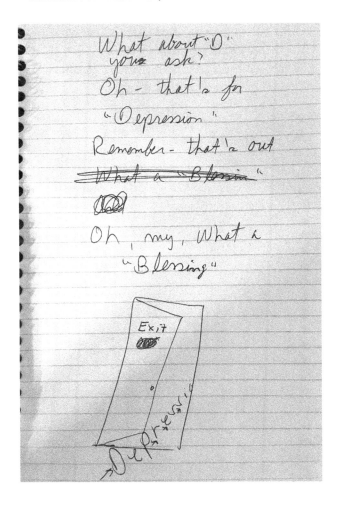

Oh, my, what a blessing!

A to Z—No "B" (Minus Three)

You'll figure this little book out real soon,
But read it anyway. It might help you;
Before—noon.

A is for Ache, we all have some.
       Remember no "B"
C is for Ceasing to stop and become a bum.
D is for Dandy, Delightful Day.
E is for Everything going your way.
F is for Feeling Fit as a Fiddle.
G is for Giving all you've Got to the middle.
H is for Healing—it might take a while.
I is for "I can't take this. Just float me down the Nile."
J is for Jockeying around with your joints.
K is for Kinks that hit all the points.
L is for Lightening up the load.
M is for Melting away the "code".
N is for Nourishing a ravaged bone.
O is for sOmetimes leaving it alone.
P is for Patience; that's what it takes.
Q is for Quiet prayers when the hurt aches.
R for Reserving a spot in therapy.
S is for Stretching the body so merrily.
T is for Tightness that will go away.
U is for Underneath yourself you will lay.
V is for Vim and Vigor you will feel.
W is for Wholeness you get when you heal.

X is for X-tra attention you will give.
Y is for all the Years you will live.
And Z—for the Zowie Zone you've been in.

What about B?
B is for Backache—you've all had your share.
It comes with the Blackness you feel in despair.
And also, the Boiling point your mind feels.
And don't forget the Bleakness that makes you want to kneel.
But enough about all these negative *B*'s.
There are three pretty good ones,
I hope you'll agree!

B for the Boldness God gives you today.
B for your Body He so neatly made.
AND—B for His Body He so freely gave!

So when your back DOES start to ache;
Just read this book and eat a piece of cake!

CAKE! Yikes! Isn't that one of those *C*'s?

A to Z—No "H"

A is for Albania with its snow so white.
B for the Bahamas: Their dance is outa sight!
C for all of Canada: It should have been the letter "AAAh?"
D has to be for Denmark: They really "swing and sway!"
E for Ethiopia: the one who stopped to chat.
F for Frankfort, Germany: They wear all kinds of hats.
G for (read the previous page).
H for—Oops! No "H"
I for Indonesia, Iraq, and Iran too. The people there are really cool.
　　They're just like me and you.
J for all the Japanese who make up quite a few.
K for Kilimanjaro: I love to say that name.
L for London, England: We're a little bit the same.
M for, naturally, Mexico with sombreros, Oh-so wide.
N for tiny Netherlands: There's really no place to hide.
O for Orange Beach, Alabama. (I bet you didn't see that one coming) Ha!
P for Polish sausage: from Poland naturally.
Q for Quiet Quasar: It makes you want to sneeze.
R for rockin' Rio de Janeiro, too.
S for Switzerland at night: The moon is almost blue.
T for Taiwanese people: They really are quite nice.
U for Union Station: where a ticket has a great price.
V for Vatican—as in Pope: I'm sure he'd say, "Hello."
W for the Wailing Wall: where many tears do flow.
X for X-traordinary people everywhere.
Y for Yugoslavia: They all know how to share.
And Z for Zats about it, folks!

What's that you say? What about "H"? Oh, yeah!
H is for the Hatred that seeps into our lives.
It likes to travel around the world: hovering far and wide.
We've got to figure out a way to knock it for a loop!
Or send it from here to kingdom come: with one gigantic boot!
Our world would be a better place if we take that word apart.
And bury it deep in the center of the earth
So it can never come into our Hearts—again!

A to Z—No "W"

Written in 2008 at Robert's retirement

A is for Ability, that's what it's going to take.
B is for the Bouncy step that your feet will make.
C for all the Cozy kind of times you'll surely have.
D is for a Dreamy day like a soothing salve.
E for all the Effort it will take to follow through.
F for every Fore-thought you will use because you're new
      (at this).
G is for the Good-Good years to think of from the past.
H for Having Had the time of living them so fast.
I is for the Innocence so many of us carry.
J is for the Jungle we work in; man is that ever scary!
K is for the awesome Kind of legacy you left.
L for Let us hope they know that they've been really blessed.
M for Many, Many thanks to those who worked beside you.
N for Numerous Numbers who only saw results behind you.
O for Opportunities that came your way each day.
P for Polishing off a job to enjoy your well-earned pay.
Q for all the Questions everybody always asked.
R for Reaching out to others even when you were latched.
      (it rhymes).
S for Serving others in a way that they all liked.
T for Trusting Jesus, holding on to Him so tight!
U is for that Ukulele playing sweetly still.
V is for the Victory you've climbed up like a hill.
Remember no "W"
X is for the X-tra part you play in this little story.

63

Y for Yelling all day long, "To our Father be the glory".
And Z is for the Zest you have, you know you've really craved it!
And what about that "W"? You guessed it—WORK.

You've Finally Made It!

So take this time to rest and relax.
And do whatever you want to.

Enjoy the way the sun comes up
And makes the sky blue—blue!

Enjoy your chair, your fan, your remote.
They all will make you cuddle.

And when your head falls back on the couch
You know you are in the snuggle (mode).

Ride your bike over and through.
It really fits your style.

Making the wheels go round and round,
Smiling all the while.

Comradery with your coffee group,
They really like to chat.

And visit your mother at her house
Until she tells you to scat!

And know that I, your wife, and friend
Am happy for you—so!

That I will join you before too long.
And off together we'll go.

This little jaunt initiated a series of "cousin" reunions. Centered around the matriarchs' birthdays and continued even after their passings.

Maryellen printed an illustrated book to accompany this story.

Written in 2009 for Mother's 90th Birthday Party

There was a baby named Laura.
A sea turtle brought her to shore-a.
She looked up and smiled.
He thought for a while.
Then kissed her and said, "They'll adore ya."

There was a little girl named Laura.
She loved her two sisters—for sure-a
They wandered all over the island with giggles.
And lived a life wholesome and pure-a.

There was a young woman named Laura.
She fell madly in love with a sail-a.
They talked and they walked until one day they "notched." (got married)
And stayed right here in lovely Flor-i-da.

There was a forty-plus something named Laura.
Her kids were babies no more-a.
One in college—away; one a sailor at bay.
The third going out to explore-a.

There is a grandma named Laura.
All her grandchildren she does adore-a.
Seven in all with kids and/or dogs.
They love their dear grandma named Laura.

There's an elderly woman named Laura.
She loves her house and her horse-a.
Her neighbors are great, make no mistake.
She's blessed from corner to corn-a.

Our hats off to you, Lady Laura.
You're finished and growing no more-a.
Thanks for your party, you ninety "old" smarty.
Now a Mellow Corn-a we'll pour-ya!

In loving memory of
Juanita B. Ehrenfeld

Born
Tuesday, March 22, 1927
Columbus, Ohio

Died
Monday, February 14, 2011
Port Charlotte, Florida

83 years, 10 months, 23 days

Services
Kays-Ponger & Uselton Funeral Home
Port Charlotte, Florida
Friday, February 18, 2011
1:00 p.m.

Officiating
Pastor James Ammerman

Final resting place
Restlawn Memorial Gardens
Port Charlotte, Florida

Arrangements entrusted to
Kays-Ponger & Uselton Funeral Homes and Cremation Services
"Every life has a story"

A mother-in-law is a woman named Juanita.
She lived her life always striving to please ya.

Six of us were privileged to use that title.
And each of us learned something from her style.

Her quiet reserve was always very loud.
And she's the one who stood out in "the crowd."

Even when her life was topsy and turvy,
She silently prayed, "God, please help me always be worthy."

And when times really were on the brink of disaster,
She'd pray harder and harder, faster and faster.

No matter what might be around the corner.
She'd always be ready, like a million-dollar performer.

From her, I hope to always be "forgiving."
Never say, "No," and to keep her kind of living.

Patience, kindness, and loving were her way
Until Monday—when she shouted, "This is my day!"

HELLO, JESUS!

September 2014, Mom's birthday bash at the Chesterfield in Palm Beach, Florida

Now she's ninety-five—Wow!
And we are all so young—not!
Can you believe at this old age,
A person can be so loved?

It all boils down to just a few things;
Our health, our faith, our love.
And to the One who made us all.
The God of heaven above.

His mastermind put all of us here—
Today—in this one place.
To celebrate one little life,
And bring us face-to-face.

A family has a lot of quirks;
As we are well aware.
But to live this long and be this loved
Is something to compare—to:

Sand in our toes and tar on our feet.
And Papa Dot enjoying a dark ale—sweet!
To:

Guava juice dripping from a sack.
And sunburn ravaging all of our backs—ouch!

Gathering in the Palm Beach house
On Christmas bright and sunny.
Waiting for Grandpa to gather us 'round,
And count out all that money.
To:

Sleepovers in the big bedroom
And toast in the toaster with "doors."
I can't ever remember a speck of dirt
On any of those beautiful floors.

We all have many, many thoughts about Palm Beach.
Way back then and now.
Wouldn't it be nice if this same love
Could GLOW ON THE WORLD SOMEHOW?

Robert's 69ᵗʰ Birthday—2015

It takes a man to love a woman.
　It takes one woman to love HER man.

It takes that man to teach HIS woman.
　　It takes that woman to learn from HER man:

　How to love.
　How to live.
　How to laugh.
　How to cry.

　Well done, my good and faithful Robert.
　Thank you, and I'm blessed to share your birthday with you!!

　　　Love,
　　—Your woman

Our Anniversary—
December 29, 2015

You used to be my "Never-Man." Never to be found.
Never to be in my life; or never to make a sound.

Then one day, you entered into my life, just like our God had planned.
And now, instead of "never", you're my "Ever-Ever" man.

I want to tell you here and now, just why I'm writing this letter.
To let you know with a great big bow; that every day is better:

Better than any day before, in every kind of way.
And every moment, I take a breath, I'll always be here to stay!

Jesus was born in Galilee, some Christmases ago.
He said, "I must do all I can do," to let Robert and Nancy know.

To let them know how much I care for both of them every minute.
And then to tell them about my life; that I really want them in it.

When everything is said and done. When they are old and gray.
I'll thank them for knowing who I am; and for living lives my way!

Written May 28, 2016

May 28th, 1965—the Day We met

It was a Saturday, your senior year.
You up in that town, me down right here.

There was a dance at the church up there.
How were we going to get there? Do we dare?!

Yes, we dared! And drove my brother's car.
It seemed too long; and very far!

We walked into that little church—unknown.
And soon, the whole room absolutely shown!

Peggy saw Carl, they started to dance.
Your eyes met mine, and my heart did prance!

Something "clicked" inside each of us.
And we knew right away we'd make quite a fuss!

Fifty-one years later, we're still side by side.
And best of all; we've let God be our guide.

He put us in that small little church that night long ago,
So we wouldn't have to search—ANYMORE!

Happy anniversary, love!

January 28, 2017

You, Lord, are the King of kings, and Lord of lords,
The Alfa and Omega. the Beginning and the End.

Your love for me is everlasting; on and on, it goes.
My love, my life, my all in all, my forever friend!

You know each thought that comes to mind.
Whether good or bad.

And when I think I'm oh-so great,
That makes you kind of sad.

Sad, because that's not the way you want me to behave.
You want me to be humble, true, and very, very brave.

Brave when persecution comes. brave to tell the truth.
And brave enough to tell the world the love they have for you.

June 2017

My life is in your great big hands, Lord. You are in control of every minute, every hour, every day, etc. My praise for you is overflowing. Thank you for loving us, your children. Thank you for your word. Your book leads me daily. It inspires me to pray for and, somehow, tell others all about you. Thank you for sending you, Holy Spirit, to grab our hearts and make them brake for what brakes yours! For giving us insight, wisdom, and courage to live on this earth as your faithful servant. Amen and amen!

Written December 2017. We were in Germany visiting Joe and his family. This announced our Christmas present to their family.

We flew across the big blue sea
To be with our other fam-i-ly!

The trip was long, as you all know.
And finally, the plane came down real low.

It landed in Germany. Frankfurt, for sure.
And there was our son, so handsome and pure.

He swept us away in his Mini Cooper.
The scenery so neat, and the ride was super!

We were going to cruise while we were here.
But those plans have changed; we'll be staying near.

So this small group of people who move all about.
Can think and pray to figure it all out.

To adjust to the order (Uncle Sam's) and ready themselves
For another deployment; with shouts and yells.

Though Christmas time here is a little strange,
We are with family and not out of range

For God to watch over us and bless us, too.
He gave His Son for me and you.

So long story short, you won't see a package.
But Dad and Mom want you to bring your baggage—

To Ehrenfeld—where our roots were born.
The hotel's on us, where we'll all be warm!

For Tara's birthday, April 9, 2018. She and the kids were in Germany while Joe was in Seoul, Korea, on deployment.

The minute I heard the horn blast that day
I knew right away, you were here to stay.

2000 was the year I believe.
Now eighteen years later, our love still received.

With each passing day, that love, it grows stronger.
You make our life happy; we have sadness no longer.

As wife to our son, you've made his life whole.
As a mother you shine, sometimes bearing your soul!

And your love for our Father shows at first glance.
He loves how you walk; He loves how you dance.

You weave in and out of whatever comes at you.
Knowing all the while, through it all, He will get you!

Written for Joe's fortieth birthday card. He was in Seoul, South Korea, on deployment from Germany, in April 2018. Tara sent him forty birthday cards from family and friends.

"Little Joe I want," he said.
Kissed dad goodnight and went to bed.

That's how you got your name, you know.
Your brother Rik—he said so.

You grew and grew all blond and tan.
Until you stopped and became a man.

Along the way, at fifteen years
You prayed to God through happy tears.

You asked Him to forgive your sins.
To come inside you and be your friend.

He said, "Yes, of course, little Joe.
I'll do more than that, I'll help you grow.

You and I have a story to tell
About my son who is alive and well.

I'll be with you every day of your life.
School, football—even finding your wife.

The one I picked the day she was born.
To be your love; a bond never to be torn.

And how do you like those kids of mine?
Twelve, nine, and four. They're mighty fine.

As a father, you shine; every trial I find
You handle as my son does all the time.

Oh, yes, there is yelling. I yelled at those men.
I overturned tables and went at 'em again."

Through years, you still go; and closer you grow
To God your creator; He loves you so.

You've committed yourself to stand up for what's right.
No matter the cost you're ready to fight.

To say what is true
With words—many-or-few.

Your mind is alert; your perception is wild.
Methodically calculating; no longer a child.

So, my son, I am so very proud.
Can you hear the applause? Can you hear the crowd?

They're yelling and cheering and having a ball.
Wishing you happiness; but most of all:

Thanking you for being "Little Joe."

I wrote this when thinking about work, or NOT work
Wednesday, January 22, 2019

"Should I stay, or should I go?"
That's what I really want to know.
Stay and keep my license real;
Go; my career forever sealed.

Do I keep a piece of paper
And know it's not just vapor?
Or cut the ties completely
And say, "Goodbye," so neatly.

Lord, thank you for your answer.
As sound as Dancer and Prancer.
You make my mind up smoothly.
Your command, I will follow truly!

Amen

Today is December 26, 2020. I renewed my license until April 30, 2022. Nancy Ehrenfeld, RN

Written soon after Eileen's passing in August 2019. Mother's sister, the other matriarch of the cousins' reunions.

Three young girls on the island of Palm.
Life so simple, life so calm.
Rode their bikes, ran, and swam.
Through coconuts on the road
With a great big WHAM!

Jimmy and Mary, their dad and mom.
He painted the Breakers,
She jellied and jammed.

They lived in a cottage
A few blocks from the ocean.
The waves rolling in and out
With a constant motion.

The name of their street
Was Park Avenue.
They lived at number 222.

So life went on till three girls
were grown.
Married with children and
out on their own.

Helen became ill and passed away.
But not until after they
Flew all the way

To England and Ireland,
their heritage lands.

To pay tribute to their parents
And the English/Irish clans.

Then there were two:
Laura turned ninety
So we asked her this question.
What do we give you?
Any suggestions?

"I'd like to visit Palm Beach again.
And see our old place,
The ocean, and sand."

So a few of us girls
Traveled with much glee,
And stayed in a quiet B&B.

Just a few blocks away
Was that Park Avenue.
And that little cottage
At 222!

Well, the numbers were there
By the new front door.
It was a big square box,
And looked like a store!

I hope it's a real home
To a fine family.
One that enjoys each other
And the house by the sea.

We drove around town,
Laughed, and had a good time.
Reminisced about life.
Adding another line—to our story.

Along came another birthday,
Eileen this time—ninety she turned.
And the Breakers did fine!

What a party she had
Her whole family was there.
Paying tribute to their matriarch
For whom they greatly cared.

Hats off to her.
To the beach, she did go.
Pulled on her swim cap
And along the shoreline did flow.
One stroke, two strokes

Until I lost count.
All eyes on her now,
Then the beach she did mount.

Everyone cheered and clapped
And said, "Way to go".
The party was ended
So home we all drove.

But wait; they're not finished.
Those Dalton girls thrive.
A few years later
Laura turned ninety-five!

We booked the Chesterfield
With a beautiful venue.
One block away
From Worth Avenue.

Small, but so stately.
It suited us well,
By making even more
Stories to tell.

We all met in the lobby
And each took our turn.
At one of the desks
With beautiful ferns.

My turn came
    And Mom (Laura) sat with me.
    I had asked for adjoining rooms
        So near us, she would be.

    The clerk gave me MY room card.
        Then said (as if she knew)
    "Here's your card, Mrs. Hooker,
            you're in room 222."

And so it goes
One year, then another.
Laura passed away—
Ninety-six was her number.

And then there was one.
Ninety-five was Eileen.
Always prim, always proper.
        And to my knowledge,
She never used a walker.

August eleventh was the day
God did choose.
And He took her—you know—
            At 2:22.

December 2019, Christmas notes to our two sons and families

Dear Joe,

I want to thank you for your never-ending support for me. You have been my friend since I first met you as a young boy. Use this gift for your enjoyment when you return to the USA.

—Love, Mickey

Dear Tara,

You and I go way back! And I really appreciate being a part of your life! The USA is so excited that you'll be back soon. You are amazing to me.

—Love, Minnie

Dear Josiah,

Hi! Just think; I'm almost sure we met fourteen years ago. That was the beginning of a great friendship! See you next summer—back in the USA.

—Love, Donald

Dear Makayla,

I knew the minute I saw you that we will be forever friends! Thank you for visiting me everywhere! You're on your way to the USA.

—Love, Daisy

Dear Joshua,

I remember every single time we saw each other at the parks! Thank you for laughing with me and waving with your "thumbs-up." Can't wait to see you back in the USA.

—Love, Goofy

Dear Rik,

Here is a little something that will help with "who knows what?" Use it knowing that it came to you from the two of us! God blessed us when He gave us you!

—Love, Dad and Mom

Dear Bobbiejo,

We hope you enjoy this bit of love in a monetary state and also that we are very blessed that Rik has you as his mate!

—Love, Dad and Mom

December 30th, Monday 2019

You want me to write
So give me a pen.
Someday I'll get started.
Who knows where; who knows when.

You want me to tell of
Your truth and your power.
The way you are with us
Each minute. Each hour.

Keeping us staid on the
Path you have chosen.
Never wavering, wandering;
Or solidly frozen!

You want me to say all
The words that are right.
All the words that will
Show us your beautiful light.

It shines, oh-so brightly
On this very dark earth.
Please help us to see it
For all that it's worth.

Now let me write about my career.
The one you had planned
Before I was here.

When playing with my doll
I emptied the box.
All the Band-Aids were used
On each "chicken pox."

I looked up from my "patient."
Dad and Mom were looking down.
So from that moment on
My lifework was found.

But when I was ten
The horse was my hero.
All kinds of statues;
I could have been Nero.

Then in high school and college
Rocks were my pleasure.
Collections and field trips,
Oh, my, what a treasure!

Fossils, too, were so fascinating.
Digging and shoveling
We just knew
Something was waiting.

The famous archeologist
Was on her way—
Or so she thought.

BUT

"My thoughts are not your thoughts.
Neither are your ways my ways," declares the Lord.
   (Isaiah 55:8)

So low and behold, the
Very year of graduation;
My AA in hand with
Many an expectation—

You stand face-to-face
With me here on the ground.
"Oh, no you don't," you tell me.
"To nursing school, you're bound."

So my doll came to life
With eyes that were seeing.
One to comfort and care for,
A real human being.

Each day that has passed
You have given so much.
Time, patience, and strength;
Discernment and such.

And while "nurse life" was happening,
So was the other.
The one with the husband,
A boy and his brother.

A wonderful, beautiful wife
    "Motherhood."
Getting as close to me as
    You could!

The "ins" and the "outs"
The "Round-a-bouts."
The ups and downs;
The Silence and Sounds.

You knew every minute,
Every second or "nano."
Just like a maestro
At his piano.

Sometimes—no, MANY times,
I wasn't even aware
Of your presence around me
Although you were there.

So, "Thank you," seems too short
And much too simple.
A drop in the bucket,
A tiny dimple!

Please know that what
I want most of all;
Is for some other little girl
To take "care of her doll."

Some prayers thrown in the mix

Friday, January 24, 2020

Father, I thank you for everything.
You make me glad; you make me sing.

Without you, I am nothing at all.
With you, I'm as wordy as Paul.

Words will come, and words will go.
The ones YOU want, I need to know.

To write them down in black-an-white;
That maybe someone will see the light!

The light you shine on them for sure,
To melt their heart and make them pure.

    Amen!

Early 2020—written in response to Dawn's idea for small group homework. Then in November, Dawn (at fifty-two) lost her battle with cancer. Her response was beautiful; I wish I had a copy.

GOD made me, no one but He.
It was He alone who created me.

God MADE me; formed me out of love and care.
Molded, shaped, and then He stared
At my sky blue eyes and short brown hair.

God made ME; me, myself, and I.
A name called Nancy—from the first little cry.

So this is what it means, you see, to say the words:
GOD MADE ME

While I jog, so many sights and sounds come before me. So as I see the names of streets and pray about the people who live in these houses and neighborhoods, my imagination runs wild. Then WRITTEN word develops.

My Jog

Monday, March 23, 2020

I traveled west on to the Big Rampart to the City of Nuremberg, where my padre introduced me to his friend Umber. Then, we picked up Rupert, and they took me to the weird colony of Razorbill. Down the road a bit lived Olancha, a nice lady who offered to share her Vermouth. Her friend Babbett came along. And we all sat down and watched *Paladin*, the old TV Western.

After a while, I continued my journey passing the huge Village of Ojibway and the tiny Village of Tidy. It all reminded me of the beautiful terrain along the Aegean Sea.

Then I left Nuremberg and jogged back to the Big Rampart and home.

My Jog

Saturday, March 28, 2020

So having gone in the western direction on Monday, today I decided to go east on the Big Rampart to the east side of that large city of Nuremberg.

One of the first surprising experiences is the interesting Spanish neighborhood of Olla. Very friendly people.

Not too far from there is the French subdivision of Lacrosse. The whole town was out playing or watching the game. The Kidron Valley is actually divided into two by this French quarter. And on the edge of the subdivision is (believe it or not) the very British hamlet of Wassail.

Next was that beautiful long isle that I had gone to on Monday. It still reminded me of the gorgeous Terrain along the Aegean Sea.

But today, I didn't pass the TINY village of Tidy. I learned on my visit that it's really NOT so tiny. A huge mountain loomed upward, looking exactly like Saint Helena!

Next in this very diversified metropolis was the strange Swedish retreat of Ojibway, where the residents really loved hearing the Odyssey recited by Casey, the mayor.

Suddenly, I discovered I had made it to West Nuremberg and the familiar areas I had enjoyed on Monday.

Tuesday, March 31, 2020

Today's venture: east on the Big Rampart to an old Indian village of Mazatlan along the Onondaga trail. The Peterborough Russian neighborhood is next; with its quaint English Chesterfield Hotel.

Onward we go to Amarillo with its huge pagoda at the center of town. Finally, we reach Rio de Janeiro; that complex, colorful city. Toward the south of the city, Hong Kong appears with Taipan and Taiwan. Very lively and friendly people.

Continuing east, we arrive at Calcutta and its abundant vineyards. That mysterious resort area is next to Mauritania, filled with gorgeous fresh fruits and vegetables of all kinds.

So now we head west on the Bridgewater dike to Damascus and past his royal highness's New Castle.

Well, back to Rio de Janeiro's center, we hike west on the Big Rampart, back to our beautiful home of Heritage Lake Park.

Thursday, April 2, 2020

This trip takes me west on the Big Rampart to the southern route of Luther. Kind of a "negative" impression comes to mind with a name like that. But "lo and behold!" Toward the end, where the community of Hampton Pointe exists, the Great Cross comes into view! The Church of the Cross is its home. High in the big blue sky, it towers above you. It brings light to the end of the tunnel. Hope in the middle of chaos!

Epilogue: But in all my travels and adventures, gazing at all the amazing, surprising, weird, marvelous sights, I discovered the truth.

The truth that it's the PEOPLE. The people are the backbone of every single village, city, metropolis, burg, isle, and neighborhood.

As I traveled, I thought of them. I thought about their beginnings, their careers, their families, their thoughts, their dreams, and their desires. Are they healthy and strong? Or sickly and weak? Rich and happy? Or poor and sad? How do they feel about their life? Did they accomplish enough? Are they young and just starting out in a new marriage? Babies, toddlers, elementaries, preteens? Or did they NOT accomplish enough?

Do they realize that there is only One True God? The God that created every little part of their being? A God who knew them before they were born!

It's amazing that all these people and all these places are part of our world even today. They work, they play, they breathe, they eat, they interact with one another; or DON'T. They wake up each morning and go to sleep each night.

My prayer for each one is that they yield to you, God. That they hurt for what hurts you. That they are sad when you are sad. My prayer is for them to have a personal relationship with you, God. And know that you have a plan for them, a plan to prosper them, not to harm them.

Amen!

Tuesday, September 1, 2020

Good morning, God. This is Nancy, your child. Thank you for creating us for your pleasure and your purpose. Thank you for loving us unconditionally AND loving us BEFORE we even knew who you are! You are an awesome God. Please turn our hearts to mush. Please break our hearts with what breaks yours. Please keep us focused on you. Do not allow us to turn to the right or turn to the left. Keep us strong in the Word. Yet let us be gentle when witnessing WITH your word. Actually, please put your words in our mouths before we speak so that when we open our lips, YOUR words will calmly and gently flow out. Open our ears to hear you LOUD and CLEAR!

Thank you for keeping Robert and me safe and healthy. Our friends and their families. Rik and Joe and their families. Continue to squelch this wicked, invisible liar of all lies (coronavirus). Annihilate every aspect of his insults, threats, and fiery arrows aimed at your children. Your kingdom. Put a hedge of protection completely around us.

Thank you again, also, for bringing Tony and Tami into our lives. They love you. You connected them with their new home. Be comfortable there. Be present in every drop of paint. In every piece of furniture, every picture on the walls. Keep their relationship close; even though they are miles apart. Let Tony's next two and a half years be rewarding and fulfilling.

Knowing that he is helping students who will become adults. Who will be in charge; who will be "our country." Thank you.

Now, Lord, as you know, Lydia has applied to live at Fountain Court. Robert and I will accept your decision. Thank you for healing her body and bringing her to her present health. You know what path she is to choose. Let her see that path clearly. And go forward in it. Thank you for listening. Amen and amen!

September 21, 2020

The birth of my husband
Of fifty-two years (and nine months)
Is the twenty-first day of September.

That's Monday, today, the
First day of the week.
The greatest of days to remember!

I met him when he was a mere child—eighteen.
Celebrating twelve years of school!
The year was 1965
A year that was OH-so COOL!

He swept me off my sixteen-year-old feet.
He took me to a dance.
And then he kissed my seventeen-year-old lips.
My heart did not have a chance!

All those years have come and gone,
But where did they all go?
Working and raising two wonderful sons,
And living that really shows
One second, sixty seconds,
One minute or five.
Each part of his life
Has been blessed

By God Himself
The three in one.
And not just by request.

At times, I'm sure
Robert asked God
To rescue him from
His trials.

But most of the thousands
And millions
Of times.
He did it with a smile.

Oh, did I mention the
Number of years
That Robert has been
On this earth?

It's been seventy-four!
Seventy-four years since
Robert's spectacular birth!

Love, your young "blond,"
blue-eyed girl!
Have a wonderful day!
—Nancy

This was written on October 7, 2020. Josiah's birthday was July 15, 2020. The family was in Germany in the midst of returning to the states. THEN, they had to wait for the completion of their new home in Pensacola. With a PERMANENT address. He will be sixteen next July 15, 2021. The birthday card that we sent spoke of getting a "bowl of grits, some other crazy stuff, and a 'CAR.'" So we included a fifty-dollar check and this note.

Deposit in the bank with the highest rate.
Almost a year away, it'll be hard to wait.

But with all that interest accruing so fast.
Before you know it, you'll have your first—

TANK OF GAS!

Christmas 2020, to Rik and Family

This card is for every single member of the clan.
It tells of our Heavenly Father's big plan!

To save us from sin; to pardon us all.
Even after Adam and Eve made their great fall!

One gift card is Dad's; Merry Christmas to you.
We're glad you are able to be with your "crew."

Another is one hundred dollars for the mom of the house.
If she wants, she can buy a car or a mouse.

The third and the last is twenty-five dollars.
It's for the "baby," the twelfth-grade scholar.

Grandpa and Grandma love you all much.
And pray that you have a blessed year—

With God's touch!

PS. Accidently mixed cards up; so good luck finding which one belongs to you!

December 25, 2020

God sent an angel
To Mary so young.
"My Holy Spirit is
Giving you a son."

You will name Him Jesus.
Emanuel, too.
"God will be with us,
With me and with you.

Well Joseph, her fiancé,
Didn't know what to think.
He loved her so much.
His heart was about to sink.

How could this be?
I know what I'll do.
I'll divorce her quietly.
She'll agree to that too!

But along came Gabriel.
The same dude with Mary.
"Go ahead and marry her,
she's not carrying your baby.

"I'm sure of that," he tells Gabe.
We haven't been together.
But what about someone else?
She's a "beaut" in any weather.

Gabriel says, "I agree with you, Joe."
But she's having GOD's Son,
Just so you know."

And you know the rest.
Nine months later;
Born to us all
Is Jesus our SAVIOR!

Written in honor of Renee Massolio who passed away at the age of fifty-one after a year's battle with colon cancer. February 7, 2021

You want me to write, so give me a pen.
Someday I'll get started; who knows where, who knows when.

You want me to tell of your truth and your power.
The way you are with us each minute, each hour.

Keeping us staid on the path YOU have chosen.
Never wavering, wandering; or solidly frozen!

You want me to say all the words that are right.
All the words that will show us your beautiful light.

It shines, oh-so brightly on this very dark earth.
Please help us to see it for all that it's worth.

That poem, written on December 30, 2019, is a preface to a lengthy story about my career using poetic justice. A career that spans over fifty years now. That's why it's so lengthy.

Career, lengthy, longevity. So upon reflection—if I got the privilege of working, laughing, loving, and living all these years, why not Renee? Why won't she be here to celebrate her sixtieth, seventieth, and eightieth birthday? Why won't she be here to see a grown Savannah fall in love and marry? Why won't she be here to witness the miracle of a grandchild? And lastly, why won't she be here to grow old beside Tom? You might be wondering about the answer to these questions. I don't know. But I DO know that God keeps His promises. In the Old Testament (before Jesus was born), there was a prophet named Jeremiah. He wrote down every word that God told him to write. Chapter 29 and verse 11 says, "For I know the plans I have for you, declares the Lord. Plans to prosper you, and not to harm you. Plans to give you hope and a future." Every detail of that promise was given to Renee.

1. She prospered. You know how? God allowed her to see through creative, artful eyes. From a creative, artful mind. Every family member, coworker, friend, acquaintance; yes, even stranger also prospered by Renee's quiet, composed, thoughtful demeanor. And her kind, caring heart. Oh, yeah; God "prospered" Renee all right!
2. Secondly, He did not harm her. Cancer harmed her. Crept right into her world and took over—or so it thought!
3. But God gave Renee hope. She never lost hope. This was Renee—always hopeful; with a positive outlook and attitude. Not only in illness. Throughout her entire life.
4. And the future you asked? Yes, the future. Her future. She lived the future each and every day of her life. See; God keeps His promises.

My friend Nicole texted this response when she received this sad news. This is a paraphrase of her text. There's a Jewish tradition called "shiva." Family and friends sit on the floor, eat no meat, don't bathe, and don't go anywhere. For a week, they just mourn. For everything they miss and won't get to do with "Renee." Friends bring food and have an emotional connection with the family. Laugh, cry, reminisce; just sit so they don't have to face the winds of adversity alone. It's a healthy tradition to be given permission to press "pause" and transition to the next chapter of life deliberately and intentionally with all the stages of grief allowed to be acknowledged as acceptable expressions of humanity—while keeping in mind that God knew this was coming. He is not too weak to stop it nor too cruel to leave us to suffer alone. He is our loving wise Father with a plan to bless those who believe and trust Him. He did the work; we enter it by faith. He never wastes a hurt. He will use this experience for good—to bless you and others. If you thank and trust Him.

Yes, Tom, it's okay to be sad; it's even okay to be mad; and it's okay to cry. Jesus, overcome with emotion, wept when His good friend Lazarus died.

So ends these inspired words. I hope HE gave you comfort, joy, and hope from them.

About the Author

The name is Nancy; she isn't fancy. Seventy-three years, she's been around, writing this and that and now publishing bound. She was born in West Palm Beach and had a normal childhood. She ran around just like you in her awesome neighborhood. Uprooted to Fort Myers when she was twelve years old, she learned to adjust to strangers and wait for her future to unfold. She went to church each Sunday though not real close to God. She joined the youth and the choir. Was all that just a facade? Then she felt a connection to that Jesus dude and became more and more interested. Almost like being *wooed*. Without even knowing it, God was standing there, ready to rescue Nancy's fall and tell her He really cares. She ignored His nudges and pokes and prods. She ignored His gentle calling. But in the end, He won the war and lifted her from falling. Now she works for Him alone. He wants His story told. She prays each day and asks Him, please, to make her strong and bold. Strong to keep on writing until His story is told. Bold to put in black and white, the words that might unfold. Unfold in someone else's world. Unfold to let them see that God is the Creator King. And without Him, we wouldn't be.